CU00970459

Copyright 2022 by Dr. Archibald Johansson - .

This document is geared towards providing regard to the topic and issue covered. The publication is sold on the idea that the publisher is not required to render an accounting, officially permitted, or otherwise, qualified services. If advice is necessary, legal or professional, a practiced individual in the profession should be ordered. From a Declaration of Principles which was accepted and approved equally by a Committee of the American Bar Association and a Committee of Publishers and Associations. In no way is it legal to reproduce, duplicate, or transmit any part of this document by either electronic means or in printed format. Recording of this publication is strictly prohibited and any storage of this document is not allowed unless with written permission from the publisher. All rights reserved. The information provided herein is stated to be truthful and consistent, in that any liability, in terms of inattention or otherwise, by any usage or abuse of any policies, processes, or Instructions: contained within is the solitary and utter responsibility of the recipient reader. Under no circumstances will any legal responsibility or blame be held against the publisher for any reparation, damages, or monetary loss due to the information herein, either directly or indirectly. By continuing with this book, readers agree that the author is under no circumstances responsible for any losses, indirect or direct, that are incurred as a result of the information presented in this document, including, but not limited to inaccuracies, omissions and errors. Respective authors own all copyrights not held by the publisher. The information herein is offered for informational purposes solely and is universal as so. The presentation of the information is without a contract or any type of guarantee assurance. The information herein is offered for informational purposes solely and is universal as so. The presentation of the information is without contract or any type of guarantee assurance. Readers acknowledge that the author is not engaging in the rendering of legal, financial, medical or professional advice. Please consult a licensed professional before attempting any techniques outlined in this book.

TABLE OF CONTENTS

3

INTRODUCTION

When stomach contents such as acid or bile move back into your esophagus, we commonly refer to it as reflux. Acid reflux is a prevalent condition that affects up to 1 in 5 adult men and women in the United States. It can also affect youngsters. Despite its prevalence, the condition is frequently undiagnosed, with its symptoms misinterpreted. This is unfortunate because Acid Reflux is usually a manageable condition. However, it can lead to significant problems if not treated appropriately.

Acid reflux is frequently accompanied by painful symptoms that can degrade a person's quality of life. Heartburn is the most common symptom of Acid reflux, but it is not the only one and may also be caused by other health conditions. Furthermore, the disease may be present even if no symptoms are present. This is why the disease is frequently misdiagnosed or self-treated.

Acid reflux is a long-term condition. Even if symptoms have been brought under control, treatment must typically be continued for a long time. Acid Reflux can be efficiently treated using a variety of approaches ranging from lifestyle changes to medication or surgical procedures.

At some point in life, most people will experience typical gastrointestinal issues, such as heartburn and indigestion, which can be relieved with just a few over-the-counter medications. On the other hand, if left untreated, more serious conditions such as gastritis and GERD may develop. If suffering from any of those conditions, medical treatment, lifestyle adjustments, and most importantly, major dietary changes are required to help your stomach out. That's where we come in.

Causes and Symptoms

There are many causes that may trigger acid reflux. Here are a few of the most common risk factors:

- Eating huge meals or laying down immediately after a meal. Eating while resting on your back or leaning over at the waist.
- Being overweight or obese.

- Smoking and drinking regularly.
- Snacking at the end of the day or eating right before bedtime.
- Eating certain extremely acidic or sweet foods, such as citrus fruits, tomatoes, chocolate, mint, garlic, onions, and spicy or fatty meals.
- Taking medication, such as aspirin, ibuprofen and many other sedatives regularly.

Similar to any other disease, symptoms of acid reflux vary from person to person, from mild to severe. Thus, it is still important to be aware of the most common signs and symptoms of these conditions.

Aside from upset stomach, bloating, hiccups, cough, indigestion, and burping, other common symptoms such as heartburn, chest pain, having trouble swallowing food, inflammation, bad breath, feeling sick, or even vomiting may be present.

In addition to these complications, long-term esophageal inflammation can cause scarring, tightness, ulceration, Barrett's esophagus, and an increased chance of developing cancer.

Any manifestations of acid reflux should be handled right away. To do this, getting prompt medical assistance is highly suggested. Also, it is important to note that even after a diagnosis, symptoms may worsen, new symptoms may arise, or treatments may be ineffective.

ACID REFLUX DIET

Diet plays a critical role in the health of your gastrointestinal tract and your entire body. Since it has immediate contact with the food you consume during your meals, it is also the first system of your body to respond to anything that enters your system. As a result, following an acid reflux-friendly diet may make a significant impact on your gut's health as well as symptom treatment or avoidance.

Maintaining a healthy gut, free of any acid reflux troubles, does not have to be a tough endeavor. Making conscious decisions about your food, when you eat it, and how much you consume is essential for regulating and eventually treating your symptoms. It is important to understand, however, that the reasons for your decision will be unique to you. In addition, your choices, willingness, and a personal path will all have a significant impact on what will help you manage your symptoms.

The first step in managing acid reflux is to take control of your diet since some foods may either ease or worsen their symptoms. To construct your optimal diet, you must first determine what works best for you. As previously stated, since individual symptoms vary, not all triggers and treatments will have the same impact on everyone.

In this book, you will discover that eating healthy and appropriate for a person with acid reflux does not need you to forego all of your favorite foods. However, incorporating a few simple modifications to your diet, as implied below, may help you out.

Protein

Eggs are included in this category due to their high protein content. The majority of the fat contained in an egg is contained in the yolk. As a result, it may elicit symptoms in very sensitive persons. If you feel that eggs may cause you troubles or discomfort, limit your menu to egg whites exclusively as they are milder on your stomach.

If you like meat and fish, there is no need to be concerned since there are several ways to prepare them without ingesting excessive fat or other irritants. Serve these meals skinned, grilled, steamed, poached, roasted, broiled, or baked without the fatty component or additional oil.

It is best to remove the skin off meat before preparing and cooking it since it holds the bulk of the fat in the meat. The same is true for bones: rather than cooking with them, remove them before cooking. Always choose lean cuts of meat, such as chicken or turkey breasts, as well as lean cuts of beef or pig, wherever possible.

If you like to eat fish, you may choose from a variety of options, including salmon, halibut, sardines, mackerel, and cod. Crabs and squids may also be included in your diet, depending on your preferences. Fish and seafood are, in general, simple to digest and include a variety of nutrients, including healthy fats and vitamins. Clams should be avoided since they might irritate your stomach, promote the formation of acid and induce nausea.

Vegan forms of protein, such as tofu, tempeh, and edamame, are included in the list of low-fat protein sources that you are urged to consume as well.

It is also not recommended that you eat processed foods such as hotdogs, bacon, sausages, and bologna since they are high in fat. Aside from having a high-fat level, some food items may also include condiments or additives that might aggravate your illness even worse.

Dairy Products

In terms of nutritional density, milk and dairy products are dietary categories that our bodies need in order to function effectively. Instead of high-fat dairy products, choose low-fat, fat-free, and low-phosphate alternatives. Dairy products that are low in fat or fat-free, such as skim milk, yogurt, and mild-flavored cheeses (such as cottage cheese, feta cheese, and Stilton), are examples of such foods.

The milk made from nuts and legumes (walnut milk, almond milk, and soy milk) is all excellent alternatives to cow's milk since they contain less fat than dairy products. Numerous people also report that vegan dairy products are less intrusive on their stomachs and that they may be able to alleviate their symptoms.

The consumption of full-fat milk, yogurt, and fatty dairy products such as whipped cream and dairy-based ice cream, or strong-flavored cheeses such as Roquefort and blue cheese, on the other hand, is prohibited due to the high-fat content of these foods. Your stomach may get irritated as a result, making the symptoms worse.

Carbohydrates

Fiber-dense whole grains such as brown rice and couscous, as well as oatmeal, are rich in carbs and low in fat. This sort of food will promote stomach health and the development of beneficial bacteria in your stomach, in addition to aiding your digestive system in the digestion of the food you consume. Make certain that all grains are properly cooked; otherwise, they may be difficult to digest.

Another alternative, rich in carbohydrates, are crops such as potatoes, purple yam, and taro. They are also excellent providers of digestible fiber, providing you with the same health advantages that you would get from eating grains on a regular basis. Carrots and beets are other excellent examples of root vegetables. Make certain that the veggies are cooked before eating them. It is possible that you may wish to remove the peels and seeds to make digestion simpler and to cause less discomfort.

Fruits and Vegetables

When choosing the fruits and fruit juices to include in your meal, it is advised that you avoid very acidic or citrusy fruits and fruity drinks such as lemons and pineapples. Instead, a wide variety of non-citrus fruits such as bananas, apples, and melons should be considered.

It is better to avoid or restrict the intake of spicy, high-fat, and high-irritant vegetables and vegetable products such as tomatoes, onions, chili powder (including cayenne pepper), pepper, and any vegetable dish that has been fried or creamed in the meanwhile. Alternatively, watery vegetables such as cauliflower, celery, cucumber, and lettuce, as well as vegetables that have been steamed, roasted, or stir-fried, are the best alternatives for weight loss.

Fats and Oils

It is suggested that you minimize or totally remove saturated fat sources from your diet in order to restrict your consumption of fats and other triggers. In addition to fatty meat cuts, several kinds of oils, including palm oil and coconut oil, as well as trans-fat sources, such as processed foods, margarine, and non-dairy coffee creamers, contain significant amounts of saturated fat.

Trans fats should be replaced with healthy fat sources such as monounsaturated and polyunsaturated fats. Monounsaturated fats are typically found in olives, sesame seeds, avocados, nuts, and seeds, among other sources. It is possible to consume cold-pressed olive or avocado oil, for example. Polyunsaturated fatty acids, on the other hand, are naturally present in foods such as maize, soybeans, flaxseeds, and fatty fish.

Using non-stick cookware may help you cut down on the quantity of oil you use in your meals. It will assist you in preventing your food from sticking to the pan while using little to no oil at all.

Herbs & Seasoning

Spice up your meals by eating more natural herbs and spices to improve your dishes and omit sugar and salt from your food. Herbs and spices are very good for your health, as many of them have a high concentration of vitamins and minerals while not being too difficult on the digestive system.

Take, for example, parsley, which has a high concentration of antioxidants and has anti-inflammatory properties. Just a few of the other herbs and spices you may use to season your food are fresh basil and a couple of bay leaves; cilantro, fennel seeds; lemongrass; marjoram; rosemary; oregano; pepper; thyme; and a pinch of salt and pepper to taste.

Drinks & Beverages

When it comes to drinks and beverages, alcoholic beverages and carbonated beverages are always at the top of the list of those that should be avoided at all costs. They have the potential to increase the formation of acid in your stomach, induce bloating, and irritate your gastrointestinal system. Citrus juices, coffee, and very sweet beverages such as hot chocolate, cacao, and other similar concoctions follow close after.

For a healthy stomach, drink natural, unsweetened herbal tea, plenty of water, and non-sour juices that are free of additives to help your stomach feel better. Vegetable juices with no pulp, such as carrot juice, red beet juice, and other similar beverages, are examples of the latter.

TIPS AND TRICKS

Avoiding the meals and beverages that cause symptoms is one of the most effective strategies to cure acid reflux illness. You can also follow some of the following strategies.

Keep away from sweet, extremely oily, or acidic food so you do not irritate your stomach further, helping it to produce even more acid, which may cause you trouble.

Stop smoking. When you smoke, nicotine relaxes all of your body's smooth muscles, which includes the LES (lower esophageal sphincter). Acid reflux illness or GERD may develop if this muscle weakens, allowing stomach acids to freely enter the esophagus.

Avoid drinking alcohol. An esophageal and stomach ulcer may be caused by alcohol, which has been shown to be an irritant. Overconsumption of alcoholic beverages may also weaken the LES, leading to reflux symptoms. For those who cannot avoid it, testing out what works best for you and your body is recommended.

For a better night sleep, place blocks beneath your bed's head to elevate it at least 4 to 6 inches to help your stomach keep the acid down.

Wear loose-fitting clothing and belts so your gut can breathe and stretch while digesting food.

Start exercising. Exercising will improve your condition and enhance your stomach emptying. If you are overweight, try making dietary modifications to reduce weight.

It is helpful to the intestines to eat smaller, more frequent meals throughout the day, as well as to avoid eating within three hours before night. Do not nap right after your meal – go for a walk instead to help your body digest the food. Do not overeat. It is possible to reduce the amount of fat and carbohydrates in your meal by chewing fully and eating slowly and deliberately when eating. By adopting these approaches, you may give your stomach more time and lower the amount of labor necessary to digest the food you consume.

Eating appropriately for acid reflux does not include removing all of your favorite foods, as has been said before. It is generally possible to alleviate the discomforts by making a few easy dietary modifications to your current regimen. The goal of this book is to aid you in constructing a diet that incorporates fruits and vegetables, lean protein, complex carbs, and healthy fats, as well as other essential nutrients. Throughout the following sections, you will discover a variety of fast and simple meals that will surely help you and your gut as you work to improve your health. Take your time with it and enjoy it!

BREAKFAST RECIPES

Pears Pancakes

Prep time: 5 min	Cook time: 10 min	Servings: 2

Ingredients

- *½ cup oats flour*
- *½ tsp of grounded nutmeg*
- *1 egg whisked*
- *⅓ cup almond milk*
- *2 grated pears*
- *2 tbsp cooking oil*
- *¼ melon, peeled*
- *A handful of raspberries*

24

- *½ cup low-fat frozen yogurt*

Directions

- Combine the flour and nutmeg in a mixing bowl.
- Add milk and an egg and wish until well combined and smooth. Add grated pears.
- Grease a frying pan with oil. Reduce the heat to a minimum and fill the pan with the pancake mixture so that the pancakes of desired size form.
- Allow for about two minutes of cooking time after spreading them out on each side. Repeat with the remaining ingredients.
- Serve with melon, raspberries, and yogurt over the top.

NUTRITION FACTS (PER SERVING)

Calories	402	
Total Fat	24.4g	31%
Saturated Fat	10.6g	53%
Cholesterol	0mg	0%
Sodium	25mg	1%
Total Carbohydrate	45.4g	17%
Dietary Fiber	8.6g	31%
Total Sugars	26g	
Protein	5.4g	

Tips: Pears are full of vitamins and minerals and are not rough on your stomach. They may help with your gut and heart health, have anti-inflammatory properties and may boost your immune system.

French Toast

Prep time: 10 min	Cook time: 20 min	Servings: 4

Ingredients

- 3 eggs
- 1 cup unsweetened coconut milk
- 1 tsp vanilla extract
- ½ tsp cinnamon
- Pinch of salt
- 8 slices of whole-grain bread, thickly sliced
- 1 cup low-fat, plain yogurt
- 1 banana, sliced
- 1 tbsp honey

Directions

- Combine the eggs, milk, vanilla, cinnamon, and salt in a large mixing basin. Mix the mixture until it is absolutely smooth.
- Over medium heat, heat a cast-iron skillet.
- Soak the bread slices in the egg mixture for 30 seconds on each side or until completely saturated.
- Cook the bread in batches until golden brown, about 4 minutes per side. Continue until all of the slices have been cooked.
- Add the yogurt and bananas on top of the French toast. Drizzle the honey on top of everything.

NUTRITION FACTS (PER SERVING)

Calories	287	
Total Fat	6.5g	8%
Saturated Fat	2.2g	11%
Cholesterol	130mg	43%
Sodium	408mg	18%
Total Carbohydrate	40.9g	15%
Dietary Fiber	4.7g	17%
Total Sugars	15.8g	
Protein	16.3g	

Tips: The bread should be well soaked. You may soak thick slices of day-old (or even several days old) bread in it until completely saturated. This is a great way to use an old loaf of bread.

Couscous and Pears Breakfast Porridge

Prep time: 5 min	Cook time: 15 min	Servings: 1

Ingredients

- ½ cup of couscous
- 1 pear
- ½ lime
- a pinch of nutmeg

Directions

- Prepare the couscous according to the package directions. It usually takes about 15 minutes of cooking time in boiling water.

- Once couscous is cooked, add peeled and grated pear and mix well with a spoon. Cook for another 30 seconds (if needed, ad a few tbsp of water to moisten everything up).
- Serve in small bowls, sprinkled with nutmeg on top.
- If desired, raisins or berries may be added.

NUTRITION FACTS (PER SERVING)

Calories   209
Total Fat 0.5g   1%
Saturated Fat 0.1g   0%
Cholesterol 0mg   0%
Sodium 6mg   0%
Total Carbohydrate 45.9g   17%
Dietary Fiber 4.8g   17%
Total Sugars 7.1g
Protein 5.9g

Tips: The procedure is straightforward. Use a 1-1 ratio of water to oats/couscous instead of the 2-1 recommended by most manufacturers. The oats will absorb all of the liquid and be somewhat al dente if you use equal parts oats and water. There will be no mush.

Warming Blackberries Porridge

Prep time: 5 min	Cook time: 10 min	Servings: 1

Ingredients

- *¼ cup millet*
- *1 tbsp chia seeds*
- *10 almonds*
- *½ cup unsweetened coconut milk*
- *¼ tsp ground cinnamon*
- *¼ tsp vanilla extract*
- *Small pinch of stevia*
- *A handful of blackberries*

Directions

- Soak the millet in ½ cup of clean water overnight.
- Soak 2 parts clean water, 1-part chia seeds, and 1-part almonds overnight.
- Drain and rinse the millet thoroughly.
- In a non-stick skillet, combine millet and unsweetened coconut milk and simmer for 7 minutes, or until cracked and creamy.
- Combine the soaked almonds and chia seeds, cinnamon, vanilla essence, and stevia in a large mixing bowl. Stir in the millet once cooked.
- To serve, pour into a bowl and top with a few fresh blackberries.

NUTRITION FACTS (PER SERVING)

Calories	461	
Total Fat	21.5g	28%
Saturated Fat	5.8g	29%
Cholesterol	0mg	0%
Sodium	8mg	0%
Total Carbohydrate	57g	21%
Dietary Fiber	18.7g	67%
Total Sugars	2.4g	
Protein	13.3g	

Tips: The right milk-to-water ratio is important to make a creamy, tasty porridge. If you use too much milk, your porridge will become sticky and thick. If you don't use any milk, your porridge won't have that creamy flavor. Of course, if you don't want to use milk, you don't have to.

Sprouted Millet Crepes

Prep time: 5 min	Cook time: 10 min	Servings: 4

Ingredients

- 1 cup millet, soaked overnight
- ¾ cup pure water
- 1 tbsp chia seeds
- 1 tbsp pure 100% vanilla extract

Directions

- Before going to bed, thoroughly rinse your millet and soak it in a water-to-millet ratio of 1:2. The next morning, thoroughly rinse and drain.

- In a blender, combine all of the ingredients and blend until smooth.
- Preheat a non-stick pan with coconut oil over high-medium heat.
- Pour a small layer of the mixture into the center of the pan and swirl it around to spread it out. For flipping, the texture should be thick enough to keep its shape.
- Flip and cook the second side when the top of the crepe is no longer liquid. Repeat until all of the mixture is gone.
- Serve with sprouted nut butter, hemp seeds, fresh lemon juice, or anything else you desire.

NUTRITION FACTS (PER SERVING)		
Calories	223	
Total Fat	4.3g	6%
Saturated Fat	0.6g	3%
Cholesterol	0mg	0%
Sodium	4mg	0%
Total Carbohydrate	39.4g	14%
Dietary Fiber	6.7g	24%
Total Sugars	0g	
Protein	6.7g	

Tips: Millet becomes soft and loose as it absorbs water, eventually unraveling into long strands. Allowing your crepe batter to hydrate allows you to make paper-thin pancakes that aren't tough or chewy but don't break apart.

Almond Coconut Granola

Prep time: 10 min	Cook time: 40 min	Servings: 20

Ingredients

- 3 ½ cups buckwheat
- 1 ½ cups unsweetened coconut chips
- 1 cup almond, roughly chopped
- ⅓ cup pumpkin seeds
- 2 tbsp chia seeds
- 1 tsp ground nutmeg
- ½ tsp sea salt
- ½ cup almond butter
- ⅓ cup canola oil, melted
- ½ cup honey
- 1 tsp pure vanilla extract

Directions

- Preheat the oven to 325°F. Set aside a large rimmed baking sheet lined with parchment paper or a Silpat baking mat.
- Combine the buckwheat, coconut chips, almond, pumpkin seeds, chia seeds, nutmeg, and sea salt in a large mixing basin.
- Combine the almond butter and melted oil in a medium microwave-safe bowl. Microwave for 20 to 30 seconds, depending on the size of the bowl. Remove the dish from the microwave and whisk until it is completely smooth. Stir in the maple syrup and vanilla extract until the mixture is completely smooth.
- Stir the dry and wet ingredients until all of the dry ingredients are nicely covered. Evenly spread the mixture onto the prepared baking sheet. Bake for 35 to 45 minutes, or until golden brown, stirring halfway through.
- Allow the granola to cool completely on the pan after removing it from the oven. When the mixture has cooled, split it up into clumps and enjoy!

NUTRITION FACTS (PER SERVING)		
Calories	185	
Total Fat	9.6g	12%
Saturated Fat	1.9g	10%
Cholesterol	32mg	11%
Sodium	170mg	7%
Total Carbohydrate	20.1g	7%
Dietary Fiber	2.6g	9%
Total Sugars	4.4g	
Protein	5.7g	

Tips: Store granola in airtight jars or containers for up to a month.

Beets Bread

Prep time: 10 min	Cook time: 40 min	Servings: 12

Ingredients

- 1 cup beets puree
- 3 eggs
- ½ cup maple syrup
- ¼ cup melted refined canola oil
- 2 tbsp stevia
- 1 tsp vanilla extract
- 1 cup coconut flour
- ½ cup tapioca flour
- 1 tsp baking powder
- 1 tsp baking soda
- 1 tsp ginger
- ½ tsp nutmeg

36

- *1 tsp cinnamon*
- *½ tsp allspice*
- *½ tsp salt*
- *⅓ cup chopped walnuts*

Directions

- Preheat the oven to 350°F.
- In a medium mixing bowl, combine the beets puree, eggs, maple syrup, melted oil, stevia, and vanilla.
- Combine the coconut flour, tapioca flour, baking soda, baking powder, cinnamon, ginger, nutmeg, allspice, and salt in a large mixing bowl. Whisk everything together until it's smooth.
- Using parchment paper, line an 8-inch loaf pan.
- Using a spatula, smooth the batter into the loaf pan.
- Sprinkle with chopped walnuts and bake for 40 minutes, or until the top is firm and springs back when pressed.
- Allow the bread to cool in the pan for 5–10 minutes before transferring it to a cooling rack by pulling the parchment paper's edges.

NUTRITION FACTS (PER SERVING)

Calories	166	
Total Fat 10.3g	13%	
Saturated Fat 1.2g	6%	
Cholesterol 47mg	16%	
Sodium 125mg	5%	
Total Carbohydrate 14.4g		5%
Dietary Fiber 3.3g	12%	
Total Sugars 5.4g		
Protein 6.1g		

Tips: Bread is best served the day it is baked, but it can be kept at room temperature for up to two days in an airtight container or properly wrapped.

Fruity and Healthy Barley

| Prep time: 5 min | Cook time: 15 min | Servings: 2 |

Ingredients

- 1 cup barley
- 2 cup water
- Generous pinch of sea salt
- ½ tbsp figs
- ½ tbsp blueberries
- ¼ tsp nutmeg
- 1 apple
- 1 tbsp sliced almonds, dry toasted
- 1 banana, thinly sliced
- Coconut milk

Directions

- Combine the barley, water, salt, figs, blueberries and nutmeg in a saucepan.
- Bring to a boil, stir well, then bring the heat to a boil. Cover and cook for about 10 minutes, stirring occasionally the barley to prevent sticking.
- While the barley is cooking, rub the apple with the thickest hole. When the barley is cooked, add the grated apple until everything is combined.
- Cover the heater and turn it off. Let the barley cook for 5 minutes.
- Serve sprinkled with sliced almonds, banana slices and a few tbsp of milk (if desired).

NUTRITION FACTS (PER SERVING)		
Calories	481	
Total Fat	5.9g	8%
Saturated Fat	2.3g	11%
Cholesterol	0mg	0%
Sodium	21mg	1%
Total Carbohydrate	99.8g	36%
Dietary Fiber	21.1g	75%
Total Sugars	21.6g	
Protein	13.3g	

Millet Muffins

Prep time: 30 min	Cook time: 20 min	Servings: 4

Ingredients

- 4 eggs
- ½ cup + 2 tbsp tomato sauce
- 1 tsp dried thyme
- ¼ tsp salt
- ⅛ tsp black pepper
- cups cooked millet
- 2 cups shredded parmesan
- ½ cup diced poblano peppers
- 2 tbsp sliced capers

Directions

- Turn on the oven to 350°F. Using non-stick cooking spray, coat a mini muffin tray.

- Whisk together eggs, 2 tbsp tomato paste, salt, and pepper in a small bowl until well combined.
- In a large mixing bowl, combine cooked millet, parmesan, poblano peppers, and capers.
- Stir in the egg mixture until everything is well combined.
- Fill the millet mixture evenly into the tiny muffin tin cups.
- Preheat oven to 350°F and bake for 15-20 min, or until golden brown. Allow 5 min for the millet bites to cool before removing them from the pan.
- Serve your millet bits and enjoy!

NUTRITION FACTS (PER SERVING)

Calories	260	
Total Fat	9.9g	13%
Saturated Fat	6.4g	32%
Cholesterol	49mg	16%
Sodium	74mg	3%
Total Carbohydrate	38.3g	14%
Dietary Fiber	12.5g	45%
Total Sugars	11.4g	
Protein	6.2g	

Tips: Egg whites include more than half of the protein in an egg, as well as vitamin B2 and less fat than the yolk. Selenium, vitamins D, B6, and B12, as well as minerals including zinc, iron, and copper, are abundant in eggs.

Breakfast Barley with Pomegranates

Prep time: 5 min	Cook time: 30 min	Servings: 4

Ingredients

- 1 cup water
- 1-½ cups coconut milk, plus more for serving
- 1 tsp vanilla extract
- 1 cup barley, rinsed well
- pinch salt
- 2 tbsp coconut sugar, plus more for serving
- ¼ tsp ground nutmeg
- ¾ cup pomegranates

- *Sliced cashews or chopped toasted walnuts for topping*

Directions

- Combine water, 1-½ cups milk, vanilla extract, rinsed barley, and salt in a heavy-bottomed saucepan. Bring to a boil over medium-high heat, stirring occasionally and keeping an eye on it to prevent it from boiling over.
- Reduce heat to low, cover with a lid that is slightly vented, and cook, stirring occasionally, for 15 minutes.
- Add coconut sugar and ground nutmeg. Place the lid back on and cook for another 5 minutes, or until all of the liquid has been absorbed.
- Remove from the heat and fold in the pomegranates gently. Serve with more coconut sugar, heated milk, and nuts on top.

NUTRITION FACTS (PER SERVING)

Calories	377	
Total Fat	20.8g	27%
Saturated Fat	6.1g	30%
Cholesterol	0mg	0%
Sodium	588mg	26%
Total Carbohydrate	39.6g	14%
Dietary Fiber	10.9g	39%
Total Sugars	1.7g	
Protein	12.8g	

Tips: Pomegranate is abundant in nutrients, including many vitamins and minerals. It may help boost your immune system and includes anti-inflammatory and anticancer properties.

Baked Apricots Hazelnuts Buckwheat

Prep time: 10 min	Cook time: 40 min	Servings: 12

Ingredients

- *2 cups buckwheat*
- *¼ cup coconut sugar*
- *½ tsp salt*
- *1 tsp baking powder*
- *1 tsp ground nutmeg*
- *½ cup chopped apricots*
- *2 cups unsweetened coconut milk*
- *1 large egg*
- *3 tbsp almond oil, melted and cooled slightly*
- *1 tsp vanilla extract*
- *¼ tsp almond extract*

- *1 ½ cups chopped hazelnuts*
- *peach slices for the top optional*

Directions

- Preheat the oven to 350°F. Set aside an 8x8 square baking dish, lined with baking paper or greased.
- Combine the buckwheat, coconut sugar, baking powder, salt, nutmeg, and apricots in a medium mixing dish.
- Whisk together the coconut milk, egg, oil, vanilla, and almond extract in a separate medium mixing dish.
- Arrange the chopped hazelnuts in the bottom of the baking dish. Pour the buckwheat mixture over the nuts in an equal layer. Over the buckwheat, pour the coconut milk mixture.
- Shake the baking dish gently to ensure that the milk is equally distributed. Add more hazelnuts on the top of the buckwheat if desired. It gives the oats a nice appearance.
- Bake for 40 minutes, or until golden brown on top and the buckwheat is set. Serve and enjoy!

NUTRITION FACTS (PER SERVING)

Calories	243	
Total Fat	13.2g	17%
Saturated Fat	8.3g	42%
Cholesterol	31mg	10%
Sodium	264mg	11%
Total Carbohydrate	28.6g	10%
Dietary Fiber	1.4g	5%
Total Sugars	15g	
Protein	4.1g	

Tips: Note that this baked buckwheat reheats well in the microwave. For added creaminess, add a splash of almond milk! To make this dish gluten-free, use gluten-free oats.

LUNCH RECIPES

Grilled Chicken Veggie Burgers

Prep time: 10 min	Cook time: 20 min	Servings: 6

Ingredients

- *1-pound lean ground chicken*
- *1 cup parsnips grated*
- *1 cup eggplant grated*
- *2 garlic cloves minced*
- *½ tsp black pepper*
- *kosher or sea salt to taste*
- *2 tsp almond oil*
- *6 slices of whole-grain bread*

- *6 romaine heart lettuce leaves*
- *1 tomato medium*

Directions

- Combine the first six ingredients in a large mixing dish and form 6 patties. Patties can be cooked on a grill, griddle, pan, or under the broiler in the oven. Cook patties for about 12 minutes over medium heat or until they are no longer pink inside.
- Brush almond oil over one side of bread pieces and broil in the oven or lay on a griddle or skillet, and cook until golden and crispy while the burgers are cooking.
- Spread your favorite sauce over the bottom part of the bread slice. Add a slice of lettuce and a slice of tomato over the patty and cover with bread. Serve immediately.

NUTRITION FACTS (PER SERVING)

Calories	211	
Total Fat	8.1g	10%
Saturated Fat	2.1g	11%
Cholesterol	54mg	18%
Sodium	246mg	11%
Total Carbohydrate	16.2g	6%
Dietary Fiber	2.9g	10%
Total Sugars	3.7g	
Protein	19.5g	

Tips: Use your favorite sauce, such as yogurt and mint sauce and vegetables, to flavor the burgers. Baked zucchini or onions, as well as freshly chopped cucumbers, taste great.

Turkey, Quinoa, & Vegetable Soup

Prep time: 15 min	Cook time: 30 min	Servings: 6

Ingredients

- 4 cups of chicken broth
- 4 cups water
- 2 ½ pounds skinless and boneless turkey breasts, cut into pieces
- 1 cup of parsnips, peeled and sliced
- 1 cup of sliced leeks
- 1 bay leaf
- 1 tsp of sea salt
- 2 cups cooked quinoa
- 1 cup of chopped green beans
- 1 cup of sliced white mushrooms

- *1–2 tbsp of fresh chopped cilantro*
- *Optional; fresh or dried thyme leaves and ⅛ tsp ground turmeric*

Directions

- In a stockpot, bring the water and broth to a boil. Add the parsnips, leeks, turkey, bay leaf, and salt. Cover and cook for 25-30 minutes, or until the meat is cooked through.
- Prepare the quinoa according to package directions.
- Add the green beans and mushrooms to the stockpot and cook for another 3-5 minutes, until all vegetables are cooked through.
- Shred the turkey with a fork after removing it from the stockpot. Reintroduce the shredded turkey to the soup.
- Remove the bay leaf from the soup, turn off the heat, and season with fresh chopped parsley, pepper, and more salt as needed. After the soup has been served, add the cooked quinoa to the soup bowl. Enjoy!

NUTRITION FACTS (PER SERVING)

Calories	206	
Total Fat	6.5g	8%
Saturated Fat	1.3g	7%
Cholesterol	37mg	12%
Sodium	841mg	37%
Total Carbohydrate	15.4g	6%
Dietary Fiber	2.5g	9%
Total Sugars	3.3g	
Protein	21.1 g	

Tips: To boost the taste of your soup or stew, add raw meat and vegetables to the pot and use fresh herbs. This way, your soup will taste fresh and delicious.

Maple BBQ Mackerel

Prep time: 15 min	Cook time: 25 min	Servings: 6

Ingredients

- *2 pounds mackerel fillets*
- *1 tbsp coconut sugar*
- *1 tsp garlic powder*
- *1 tsp smoked paprika*
- *½ tsp salt*
- *½ tsp freshly ground black pepper*
- *¼ tsp cumin*
- *2 to 3 tbsp maple syrup*

51

Directions

- Preheat the oven to 400°F. Place the fish on a baking pan (skin side down) and bake for 10 minutes.
- Whisk together the sugar, garlic powder, paprika, salt, pepper, and cumin in a small bowl. Toss it evenly over the mackerel fillets. Drizzle the maple syrup over each fillet and use a spoon to "spread" it all over the fillet.
- Roast the mackerel for further 10 to 15 minutes, or until it flakes easily with a fork. When it comes out of the oven, brush it with a bit more maple syrup if desired. Chop the chives and sprinkle over the top. Serve right away.

NUTRITION FACTS (PER SERVING)

Calories	503	
Total Fat	36.4g	47%
Saturated Fat	7.3g	36%
Cholesterol	73mg	24%
Sodium	1236mg	54%
Total Carbohydrate	7.8g	3%
Dietary Fiber	0.4g	1%
Total Sugars	6.2g	
Protein	40.2g	

Teriyaki Chicken Skillet with Vegetables

Prep time: 15 min	Cook time: 30 min	Servings: 4

Ingredients

- *2 tbsp olive oil*
- *½ red onion, finely chopped*
- *2 large parsnips, peeled and chopped*
- *1 bunch beetroots, chopped*
- *1 tbsp fresh ginger, peeled and grated*
- *1-pound ground (or finely chopped) chicken*
- *¼ cup teriyaki sauce*

- *2 medium zucchinis, chopped*
- *2 cups baby kale,*
- *½ tsp sea salt, to taste*

Directions

- In a large (12-inch) skillet with deep sides, heat the oil over medium heat. Cook, turning regularly until the red onion begins to soften, about 3 minutes. Add the parsnips, beetroots, and ginger and cook for another 3 minutes with the lid on.
- Place the vegetables on one side of the skillet and add the ground chicken to the other. Brown for 2 to 3 minutes on one side, then flip and brown for another 2 minutes.
- Mix everything together.
- Add the teriyaki sauce, zucchini, kale, and sea salt to a pan. Cover and heat for 4 to 5 minutes, or until the turkey is cooked through and vegetables are done to your liking.
- Serve with sesame seeds and minced chives.

NUTRITION FACTS (PER SERVING)

Calories	291	
Total Fat	13.7g	18%
Saturated Fat	2.3g	12%
Cholesterol	116mg	39%
Sodium	1094mg	48%
Total Carbohydrate	12.9g	5%
Dietary Fiber	3.1g	11%
Total Sugars	6.8g	
Protein	34.4g	

Tips: To begin, brine the chicken for 20 to 30 minutes in a mixture of water and a few tbsp of salt. This will enhance the natural flavor and moisture of the chicken breasts, resulting in a flesh that is extremely soft.

Cashew Turkey

Prep time: 5 min	Cook time: 20 min	Servings: 4

Ingredients

For the Sauce

- 6 tbsp coconut aminos
- 1 tbsp hoisin sauce
- ¾ tbsp apple cider vinegar
- 2 tbsp maple syrup
- 1 tsp toasted sesame oil
- ½ tsp fresh minced ginger

- *2 cloves garlic minced*
- *2 tbsp corn-starch*
- *½ cup water plus more as needed to thin out the sauce*

For the Turkey and Vegetables

- *2 medium skinless, boneless turkey breasts cut into 1-inch cubes*
- *Salt and black pepper to taste*
- *1 ½ cups broccoli florets, about 1 head*
- *1 red bell pepper cut into chunks*
- *½ green bell pepper cut into chunks (optional - for extra color)*
- *⅔ cup roasted unsalted cashews*

Directions

- To make the sauce, combine coconut aminos, hoisin sauce, vinegar, maple syrup, sesame oil, garlic, ginger, corn starch, and water in a medium saucepan over medium heat until mixed. Cook, stirring constantly until the sauce thickens and bubbles. Remove the pan from the heat and set it aside.
- To make the turkey, preheat to 400°F.
- Set aside a large sheet pan lined with parchment paper or foil.
- Season the chicken with salt and black pepper, then spread a dollop of sauce over both sides of the bird. At least half of the sauce should be saved for later.
- Cook for 8 minutes in a preheated oven before removing the pan.
- Arrange the broccoli florets, bell peppers, and cashews around the chicken in a single layer. Season the vegetables with salt and pepper, then sprinkle a tbsp of sauce over them and toss to coat. Cook for another 8-12 minutes in the oven, or until the chicken is cooked through and the juices run clear.

- Remove the skillet from the oven and pour the remaining sauce over it. Garnish with green onions and sesame seeds, if desired, and serve over rice or quinoa.

NUTRITION FACTS (PER SERVING)

Calories	176	
Total Fat	3g	4%
Saturated Fat	0.2g	1%
Cholesterol	36mg	12%
Sodium	1619mg	70%
Total Carbohydrate	21.7g	8%
Dietary Fiber	1.7g	6%
Total Sugars	12.3g	
Protein	16.8g	

Black Beans and Farro Salad

Prep time: 20 min	Cook time: 1h 15 min	Servings: 4

Ingredients

- _1 cup farro_
- _2 tbsp olive oil_
- _1 tsp garlic powder_
- _¼ cup almond butter_
- _14 oz can black beans, drained, rinsed_
- _14 oz mixed tomatoes; large ones halved or quartered_
- _2 oz baby kale leaves_
- _2 tbsp hemp seeds, toasted, to serve_
- _2 tbsp pine nuts, toasted, to serve_

Directions

- Fill a pot halfway with water and add the farro. Cook according to a package direction. Drain.
- In a screw-top jar, combine oil and garlic. Set aside after giving it a good shake.
- Place almond butter, dressing, and two tsp water in another screw-top jar. To blend, give it a good shake. The consistency should be between runny and thick.
- Place farro in a big mixing dish. Stir in the black beans, half of the kale leaves and tomatoes gently to mix. Drizzle the almond butter dressing over the farro salad.
- Toss with toasted hemp seed and pine nuts before serving.

NUTRITION FACTS (PER SERVING)

Calories	337	
Total Fat	13.2g	17%
Saturated Fat	1.9g	10%
Cholesterol	0mg	0%
Sodium	231mg	10%
Total Carbohydrate	48g	17%
Dietary Fiber	10.7g	38%
Total Sugars	2.5g	
Protein	10.4g	

Tips: Farro is a very healthy grain as it includes a lot of proteins, fiber and minerals, some of which are zinc, iron and magnesium.

Pears and Beef

Prep time: 10 min	Cook time: 35 min	Servings: 4

Ingredients

- 3 tbsp maple syrup
- ½ tsp ground cinnamon
- ¼ tsp ground nutmeg
- 1 tbsp olive oil
- 4 beefsteak (3.5 oz each)
- 1 tbsp butter
- 3 large fresh pears (peeled and chopped)
- 1 tbsp apple cider
- 3 tbsp raw chopped macadamia nuts

Directions

- In a small bowl, combine the maple syrup, ½ tsp cinnamon, and ½ tsp nutmeg.
- In a skillet, heat 1 tbsp oil over medium heat and add beef.
- Cook for 3–4 minutes on each side or until thoroughly done.
- Remove the steak from the pan and cover with foil to keep warm.
- In the same pan, melt the butter and add the maple syrup mixture. Cook for ½ minute on low heat.
- Stir in the pears and apple cider for a few minutes or until the pears are softened. Add the macadamia nuts and mix well.
- Return the steak to the pan and flip to absorb some of the pear's flavor.
- Serve stakes right away with ⅔ cup pears mixture on top.

NUTRITION FACTS (PER SERVING)

Calories	484	
Total Fat	23.3g	30%
Saturated Fat	7.5g	37%
Cholesterol	99mg	33%
Sodium	89mg	4%
Total Carbohydrate	50.3g	18%
Dietary Fiber	4.6g	16%
Total Sugars	27.2g	
Protein	22.1g	

Beef Tenderloin and Butternut Squash

Prep time: 15 min	Cook time: 4 h	Servings: 6

Ingredients

- 2-pound beef tenderloin
- 1 tsp garlic powder
- 1 butternut squash, peeled and cubed
- 1 cup turnips
- 4 cups water

Directions

- Sprinkle garlic over the beef in a slow cooker.
- Surround the meat with butternut squash and turnips. Fill the container halfway with water.

- Cook on low for 4 hours or until meat is slightly pink in the center and vegetables are soft.
- At least 145 ° F should be read on an instant-read thermometer, pinned into the center of the meat.
- Serve immediately, garnished with freshly ground black pepper and chopped herbs if desired.

NUTRITION FACTS (PER SERVING)

Calories	333	
Total Fat	13.9g	18%
Saturated Fat	5.3g	26%
Cholesterol	139mg	46%
Sodium	109mg	5%
Total Carbohydrate	5.3g	2%
Dietary Fiber	1.5g	5%
Total Sugars	1.6g	
Protein	44.3g	

Tips: Beef is high in protein, which aids muscle growth and maintains muscle mass. It also contains a lot of iron and collagen.

Eggplant and Black-Eyed Peas Bowl

| Prep time: 5 min | Cook time: 15 min | Servings: 4 |

Ingredients

- 1 ½ tbsp olive oil
- ½ cup chopped onion
- 1 tsp garlic powder
- ½ tsp curry powder
- ¼ tsp kosher salt
- ¼ tsp paprika
- ⅔ cup soy milk
- 1 tsp unsalted tomato puree
- 3 oz. fresh eggplants, cut into pieces
- 5 oz. frozen fava beans, thawed
- ¼ cup cooked black-eyed peas
- ½ cup cooked quinoa, warmed

64

Directions

- In a medium-sized heavy skillet, heat the oil over medium-low heat. Cook, stirring occasionally, until onion and garlic are soft, about 5 minutes. Stir in the curry powder, salt, and paprika; cook, stirring constantly, for about 30 seconds or until aromatic. Blend the contents in a blender, with milk and tomato puree, until creamy.

- Using paper towels, wipe the skillet clean. Preheat the skillet to high. Cook the eggplants for 3 to 4 minutes until slightly browned. Add black-eyed peas and fava beans and cook for another 5-6 minutes.

- Add the sauce and cook, stirring occasionally, until the curry sauce has thickened slightly, about 4-5 minutes. Add in the quinoa and stir. Adjust the seasoning if necessary.

- Divide the content into bowls and garnish with fresh herbs, such as basil and cilantro, if desired. Serve immediately.

NUTRITION FACTS (PER SERVING)

Calories	388	
Total Fat	14.4g	18%
Saturated Fat	2g	10%
Cholesterol	21mg	7%
Sodium	443mg	19%
Total Carbohydrate	53g	19%
Dietary Fiber	10.2g	36%
Total Sugars	9.2g	
Protein	15.7g	

Tips: Black-eyed peas may help you with digestion due to their high fiber content. They promote bowel movements, lower your blood pressure and cholesterol levels, help with weight loss and can reduce internal inflammation.

Asian Tempeh Bulgur Bowls

| Prep time: 15 min | Cook time: 30 min | Servings: 4 |

Ingredients

- 16 oz. tempeh
- ¾ cup bulgur wheat
- 3 tbsp coconut aminos
- 2 tbsp coconut nectar
- 1 tsp ginger
- 1 tbsp grapeseed oil
- 1 tsp garlic powder
- 3 cups shredded cabbage
- 1 cup shredded daikon
- ½ cup edamame
- 2 tsp hemp seeds (optional)

Directions

- To remove as much water as possible, press the tempeh between paper towels or napkins.
- Cook the bulgur wheat according to the package guidelines while the tempeh is pressing.
- In a medium mixing bowl, combine the coconut aminos, coconut nectar, and ginger. Allow the tempeh to soak in the sauce mixture for about 5 minutes after cutting it into pieces.
- Heat the oil over medium heat and softly sauté the garlic.
- Add and cook the soaked tempeh until crispy (leave the leftover sauce in the bowl), about 10-15 minutes.
- Add in the cabbage and daikon and cook for 2-3 minutes, then return the tempeh to the pan, along with bulgur.
- Cook for another 5 minutes or until everything is evenly coated and hot. Optional garnishes include edamame and hemp seeds.

NUTRITION FACTS (PER SERVING)

Calories	301	
Total Fat	12.6g	16%
Saturated Fat	2.2g	11%
Cholesterol	0mg	0%
Sodium	36mg	2%
Total Carbohydrate	31.5g	11%
Dietary Fiber	5.3g	19%
Total Sugars	5.8g	
Protein	19.9g	

Tips: Beta-carotene, vitamin C, and fiber are abundant in cabbage. Vitamin C helps to eliminate toxins, which are the main cause of arthritis, gout, and skin problems.

One-Skillet Chicken in Mushroom Sauce

Prep time: 10 min	Cook time: 45 min	Servings: 4

Ingredients

- *2 tbsp butter one to sear chicken, one to brown mushrooms*
- *1 tbsp olive oil*
- *6 chicken thighs*
- *1-pound mushrooms - sliced*
- *1 cup onion thin sliced*
- *¾ cup chicken stock*
- *¾ cup beef stock*
- *¼ cup coconut flour*
- *Salt and pepper to taste*

68

Directions

- Preheat a large skillet over high heat.
- Lightly salt and pepper chicken thighs.
- In a heated skillet, add one tbsp of oil and one tbsp of butter.
- Chicken thigh should be seared for 2-3 minutes on each side in a hot pan. Remove the thighs from the skillet and keep them warm in the oven. Reduce the heat to medium-low and add another tbsp of butter to the pan.
- Sauté the sliced mushrooms and onions until they are gently browned. Approximately 5 minutes
- In a measuring cup, combine the beef and chicken stock. Whisk in the flour until there are no lumps. Simmer until thickened in the mushroom/onion mixture. Approximately 2-3 minutes.
- Reduce the heat to low-medium. Return the chicken thighs to the pan and cook for a further 10 minutes, uncovered. Make sure everything is finished. The chicken thighs are done when the internal temperature reaches 145 degrees.

NUTRITION FACTS (PER SERVING)

Calories	117	
Total Fat	5.6g	7%
Saturated Fat	1.7g	8%
Cholesterol	22mg	7%
Sodium	521mg	23%
Total Carbohydrate	7.2g	3%
Dietary Fiber	2.1g	8%
Total Sugars	3.6g	
Protein	10.2g	

Blackened Trout

Prep time: 5 min	Cook time: 10 min	Servings: 4

Ingredients

- *4 trout fillets*
- *Sesame oil*
- *1 tbsp chipotle chili powder*
- *2 tsp basil*
- *1 tsp cumin*
- *1 tsp marjoram*
- *1 tsp garlic powder*
- *1 tsp onion powder*
- *1 tsp salt*
- *½ tsp ground black pepper*

- *½ tsp ground red pepper*

Directions

- To make blackening powder, combine the dry components in a small basin. Then, using either water or cooking spray, moisten the sides of each trout fillet and coat with blackening powder.
- In a skillet over medium-high heat, heat 1 tbsp of oil per fillet. When the oil is practically smoking, add the fillets and fry for 3 minutes per side, or until the fish is opaque and flaky.
- Remove from the pan and serve right away.

NUTRITION FACTS (PER SERVING)

Calories	398	
Total Fat	20.1g	26%
Saturated Fat	6.7g	33%
Cholesterol	145mg	48%
Sodium	359mg	16%
Total Carbohydrate	3.4g	1%
Dietary Fiber	0.1g	0%
Total Sugars	0g	
Protein	49.3g	

Tips: Serve with an Italian salad or green beans or on top of whole-wheat pasta.

Couscous Crusted Mackerel

Prep time: 5 min	Cook time: 10 min	Servings: 2

Ingredients

- *1 egg*
- *3 tbsp panko breadcrumbs*
- *3 tbsp couscous uncooked, rinsed*
- *½ tsp salt*
- *½ tsp garlic minced*
- *½ tsp cilantro*
- *2 tbsp olive oil*
- *12 oz. mackerel fillets*

- *chives for garnish*

Directions

- In one bowl, whisk the egg. In another, add the panko breadcrumbs, uncooked couscous, salt, garlic, and cilantro.
- In a non-stick skillet, heat 1-2 tbsp oil over medium-high heat.
- Each mackerel fillet should be dipped in the egg mixture and then straight into the quinoa mixture, ensuring that both sides are coated.
- Cover the skillet with a lid and place the mackerel skin-side down in the skillet. Fry for 5-6 minutes, then flip and cook for an additional 1-2 minutes.
- Serve mackerel with fresh chives on top.

NUTRITION FACTS (PER SERVING)

Calories	108	
Total Fat	0.3g	0%
Saturated Fat	0.1g	0%
Cholesterol	0mg	0%
Sodium	310mg	13%
Total Carbohydrate	24.5g	9%
Dietary Fiber	1.8g	6%
Total Sugars	18g	
Protein	1.4g	

Tips: Before putting the fish fillet into the egg mixture and quinoa, make sure it's completely dry.

DINNER RECIPES

Lentil and Cannellini Bean Soup

| Prep time: 10 min | Cook time: 35 min | Servings: 4 |

Ingredients

- 2 quarts water
- 4 ounces dried lentils
- 4 ounces dried cannellini bean
- 2 tsp. olive oil
- 4 ounces green onion (diced) (about 3 stalks)
- 4 ounces turnips (peeled and diced)
- 3 cups no salt added vegetable stock
- 1 cup water
- ¼ tsp salt

75

- *3 bay leaves*
- *fresh ground black pepper to taste*

Directions

- In a large mixing basin, combine water, lentils, and cannellini beans and set aside for at least 10 hours.
- Drain and rinse thoroughly.
- In a large saucepan over medium-high heat, heat the olive oil.
- Add the onions and cook for about 4 minutes, or until the green onion is slightly transparent. Stir the mixture constantly.
- Cook for further 3 minutes after adding the turnips. Stir the mixture constantly.
- Add the black beans and lentils, as well as the vegetable stock, water, and bay leaves.
- Reduce the heat to low and continue to cook for 45 minutes.
- Simmer for another 15 minutes after adding salt and pepper.

NUTRITION FACTS (PER SERVING)		
Calories	248	
Total Fat	5.9g	8%
Saturated Fat	2.1g	10%
Cholesterol	0mg	0%
Sodium	752mg	33%
Total Carbohydrate	39.7g	14%
Dietary Fiber	14.9g	53%
Total Sugars	6.9g	
Protein	13.2g	

Macadamia Nuts Crusted Flounder

Prep time: 10 min	Cook time: 15 min	Servings: 2

Ingredients

- 1 ½ ounces raw macadamia nuts
- 1 tbsp fresh marjoram
- 1 ½ tsp fresh thyme
- ⅛ tsp salt and freshly ground black pepper (to taste)
- ¼ tsp smoked paprika
- 1 tbsp honey
- 2 4-ounce boneless flounder filets
- 1 tbsp olive oil

Directions

- In a mini-chopper or blender, pulse the Macadamia nuts, marjoram, thyme, salt, pepper, and paprika until the mixture resembles gritty sand.
- In a small bowl, combine the macadamia nuts mixture with honey. Mix everything together until it's completely smooth.
- Preheat the oven to 375°F and place a big skillet in it, greased with 1 tbsp oil.
- Place the flounder on a small dish or chopping board, skin side down. Apply the pecan mixture equally to the flounder flesh side. Put the fillets skin side down on the pan and return the pan to the oven. Bake the fillets for 5 min on each side.
- Preheat the oven to broil – bake the fish for further 3-5 minutes, or until the crust is gently browned.
- Serve with cooked rice.

NUTRITION FACTS (PER SERVING)

Calories	474	
Total Fat	32.6g	42%
Saturated Fat	6.3g	31%
Cholesterol	82mg	27%
Sodium	212mg	9%
Total Carbohydrate	11.9g	4%
Dietary Fiber	3.2g	11%
Total Sugars	7g	
Protein	30g	

Tips: The 10-minute rule states that fish should be cooked for 10-minutes per inch of thickness. Then, halfway through the cooking period, flip the fish only once. Start by measuring the thickest section of the fish with a clean ruler, whether you want to follow a recipe or not.

Trout Mac and Cheese

Prep time: 10 min	Cook time: 60 min	Servings: 4

Ingredients

- *8 ounces gluten-free penne pasta*
- *2 large eggs*
- *½ cup coconut milk*
- *¼ tsp dried thyme*
- *4 ounces gouda cheese (grated)*
- *8 ounces trout sliced into thin strips*
- *1 cup edamame*
- *¼ tsp salt*
- *fresh ground black pepper (to taste)*

Directions

- Preheat the oven to 325°F.
- In a medium stockpot, bring the water to a boil over high heat.
- Add pasta and cook, stirring occasionally, until the pasta is slightly underdone.
- In a medium mixing bowl, whisk together the eggs and milk while the pasta is cooking. Whisk until everything is fully combined.
- Fold together the thyme, cheese, trout, edamame, salt, and pepper in a mixing bowl.
- Drain the pasta well before adding it to the mixing bowl. Combine the cheese and trout mixture in a mixing bowl and stir until fully combined.
- Place the mixture in a 9-inch Pyrex dish and bake for 30 minutes. Bake for 30 minutes. Chill before eating.

NUTRITION FACTS (PER SERVING)

Calories	653	
Total Fat	16.1g	21%
Saturated Fat	6.8g	34%
Cholesterol	143mg	48%
Sodium	433mg	19%
Total Carbohydrate	94.3g	34%
Dietary Fiber	2.2g	8%
Total Sugars	1.6g	
Protein	30.1g	

Tips: Do not rely on the package to tell you how long to cook something (this is only a guideline). Most pasta take 8 to 12 minutes to cook. During the cooking, taste the pasta to see how done it is.

Marjoram Lamb

Prep time: 10 min	Cook time: 30 min	Servings: 2

Ingredients

- 2 tbsp apple juice
- 2 tsp rice vinegar
- ⅛ tsp salt
- 1 tsp fresh marjoram leaves
- fresh ground black pepper (to taste)
- 8 ounces lamb breast
- 2 tsp olive oil
- ¼ cup cranberry juice
- 1 tsp unsalted butter

81

Directions

- Preheat the oven to 325°F and place a medium skillet in it.
- In a small bowl, stir together the juice, vinegar, salt, marjoram, and pepper. Toss the lamb in the basin to evenly coat it.
- Place the lamb in the oven after adding the olive oil to the skillet. There will be some marinade leftover; set aside the remaining.
- Roast the lamb for about 10 minutes, then turn it over and brush it with the remaining marinade before returning it to the oven.
- Roast for another 7-10 minutes, or until the lamb reaches 160 degrees Fahrenheit. Remove the lamb from the oven and set it aside to rest on a chopping board.
- Place the skillet on the stovetop over medium-high heat and deglaze with the cranberry juice. Stir continuously and scrape up any stuck-on chunks from the bottom of the pan.
- Simmer until the liquid has been reduced by half, then add the butter and remove it from the heat. Serve the butter on top of the lamb after whisking it into the sauce until it melts.

NUTRITION FACTS (PER SERVING)

Calories	373	
Total Fat	15g	19%
Saturated Fat	4.2g	21%
Cholesterol	106mg	35%
Sodium	277mg	12%
Total Carbohydrate	21.1g	8%
Dietary Fiber	0.4g	1%
Total Sugars	18.3g	
Protein	33g	

Tips: Tougher slices of lamb become fork-tender after slow simmering in liquid. The ideal cuts for slow cooking are the neck, shoulder, and belly, which should be cooked for at least 2 hours at 150°C to soften the meat.

Sweet Potato with Sorghum

Prep time: 10 min	Cook time: 15 min	Servings: 4

Ingredients

- *onion 1 large, finely chopped*
- *1 tsp garlic powder*
- *1 tbsp olive oil*
- *1 tbsp paprika*
- *2 sweet potatoes, peeled and cubed*
- *1 cup sorghum*
- *½ cup chickpeas, cooked and drained*
- *1 cup pinto beans*
- *small bunch of parsley, chopped*

Directions

- In 1 tbsp of olive oil, soften the onion and garlic in a pan over medium-high heat (it takes between 5 and 7 minutes).
- Cook for another minute after adding the paprika, then add the sweet potatoes, sorghum, and chickpeas.
- Cook, stirring occasionally, until the sweet potato and sorghum are cooked and the sauce has thickened, about 15-20 minutes.
- In another bowl, bring the beans to a boil, then remove them from the heat. Add to the other ingredients and mix well.
- Serve in a bowl after stirring in the parsley.

NUTRITION FACTS (PER SERVING)

Calories	225	
Total Fat	4.4g	6%
Saturated Fat	0.4g	2%
Cholesterol	1mg	0%
Sodium	205mg	9%
Total Carbohydrate	35.3g	13%
Dietary Fiber	8g	29%
Total Sugars	7.6g	
Protein	13.9g	

Tips: Sweet potatoes include roughly 20 net carbohydrates per medium potato. They are not the best choice to consume if you're watching your carb intake. However, they are considered very nutritious, easy to digest and do not irritate the stomach.

__Honey Tarragon Chicken Breasts__

Prep time: 10 min	Cook time: 40 min	Servings: 8

Ingredients

- *3 lb. bone-in chicken breast, rinsed and pat dried*
- *1 large onion (peeled and cut into eighths)*
- *2 tbsp fresh tarragon leaves*
- *½ tsp salt*
- *½ tsp peppercorns*
- *½ tsp dried basil leaves*
- *¼ cup honey*
- *½ cup chicken stock + more for moisture*

Directions

- Preheat the oven to 350°F. Use aluminum foil to line a roasting pan. Place the onion slices at the bottom of the pan.

85

- Sprinkle the onions with salt, tarragon, basil, and peppercorns. Cover with honey (you may also add a few tbsp of chicken stock for moisture).
- Place the chicken breast (skin side up) on top of the onions and cover lightly with aluminum foil before placing the pan in the preheated oven. Bake for 15 minutes, covered.
- Remove the aluminum foil and bake for another 20-25 minutes or until the internal temperature reaches 165°F and the liquid has somewhat evaporated.
- Allow to rest for at least 10 minutes before carving on a cutting board.
- In a blender, purée the roasted onions, herbs, and remaining liquid until smooth. To achieve the appropriate thickness, add up to ½ cup chicken stock (it might take less, but if it is still not thin enough, use a little water - about a tbsp at a time). Serve, drizzled over the chicken slices.

NUTRITION FACTS (PER SERVING)

Calories	240	
Total Fat	3g	4%
Saturated Fat	0.6g	3%
Cholesterol	73mg	24%
Sodium	1924mg	84%
Total Carbohydrate	22.6g	8%
Dietary Fiber	1.5g	5%
Total Sugars	18.5g	
Protein	29.6g	

Tips: To begin, brine the chicken for 20 to 30 minutes in a mixture of water and a few tbsps of salt. This will enhance the natural flavor and moisture of the chicken breasts, resulting in a flesh that is extremely soft. This is the only way to guarantee that your chicken will not be dry or rough.

Smoked Black Beans Spinach Stir Fry

Prep time: 5 min	Cook time: 15 min	Servings: 4

Ingredients

- 1 can of black beans, drained
- 1 small shallot, chopped
- ¼ cup chopped leeks
- 1-½ cups fresh zucchini sliced
- 8 oz cooked barley
- 2 cups fresh baby spinach
- 1 tbsp smoked paprika
- 1 tsp sea salt
- 1 tbsp garlic powder
- 3 tbsp olive oil
- red pepper flakes

Directions

- Over medium-high heat, heat the oil.
- Stir-fry the black beans, leeks, shallot and zucchini for 3 minutes until they've softened. Season with salt and spices.
- Stir in the fresh spinach and barley and cook 2-3 minutes, until everything is warm.
- Red pepper flakes can be added as a finishing touch.

NUTRITION FACTS (PER SERVING)

Calories	360	
Total Fat	12.6g	16%
Saturated Fat	1.9g	9%
Cholesterol	0mg	0%
Sodium	543mg	24%
Total Carbohydrate	55.5g	20%
Dietary Fiber	3.6g	13%
Total Sugars	2.5g	
Protein	8g	

Tips: Spinach has a low carbohydrate content but a high insoluble fiber content. This type of fiber could help with digestion.

Fish Soup with Sweet Potatoes

Prep time: 10 min	Cook time: 20 min	Servings: 4

Ingredients

- *1 tbsp olive oil*
- *1 large onion (diced)*
- *2 leeks (diced)*
- *1 large carrot (peeled and diced)*
- *16 ounces sweet potatoes (peeled and diced)*
- *5 cups water*
- *1 tsp apple cider vinegar*
- *2 bay leaves*
- *½ tsp dried thyme*
- *¼ tsp salt*
- *fresh ground black pepper (to taste)*

89

- *2 cloves garlic*
- *16 ounces tuna*

Directions

- In a medium stockpot, heat the oil over medium heat. Cook, stirring regularly, for about two minutes after adding the onions. Cook for two minutes after adding the leeks and carrots. Cook for one minute after adding the sweet potatoes.
- Combine the water, vinegar, bay leaves, thyme, salt, and pepper in a large mixing bowl.
- Peel and smash the garlic, but do not chop it. Toss the two garlic cloves into the saucepan. Reduce the heat to low and keep the soup simmering. Cook for 45 minutes, stirring occasionally.
- Add the fish to the soup, cut into 1-inch cubes. Cook for 20 minutes more. Before serving, take out the garlic cloves and bay leaves.

NUTRITION FACTS (PER SERVING)

Calories	383	
Total Fat	10.6g	14%
Saturated Fat	2.9g	15%
Cholesterol	35mg	12%
Sodium	238mg	10%
Total Carbohydrate	38.4g	14%
Dietary Fiber	6.3g	22%
Total Sugars	3.3g	
Protein	32.6g	

Tips: Place the fish in a wire basket in the saucepan and submerge it. Allow the water to return to a boil, which may take 2 to 3 minutes, and then cook the fish until it can easily be flaked with a fork, which should take 10 to 12 minutes.

Coconut Parsnips Soup

Prep time: 20 min	Cook time: 40 min	Servings: 2

Ingredients

- ½ tbsp olive oil
- 1 small yellow onion, chopped
- 1 tsp red curry paste
- 1 tsp ginger powder
- 1 pound's parsnips, peeled and cut in into ½-inch pieces
- Salt, to taste
- 1½ cups water
- 1½ cups vegetable broth
- 1 cup coconut milk
- basil, for garnish

Directions

- In a medium saucepan, heat oil over medium to high heat. Add the onion and cook for 5 minutes or until translucent. Add the curry paste and ginger. Stir for 2 minutes.
- Add the parsnips and a generous pinch of salt. Cover the Parsnips and let them steam for 5 minutes, stirring occasionally. Cover and add water and broth and coconut milk. Bring to a boil. Cover and simmer for at least 30 minutes or until the carrots are tender.
- Puree the soup until very smooth. Heat and add more water if the soup is too thick. Serve with cilantro sprigs.

NUTRITION FACTS (PER SERVING)

Calories	384	
Total Fat	28.4g	36%
Saturated Fat	21.8g	109%
Cholesterol	0mg	0%
Sodium	914mg	40%
Total Carbohydrate	32.3g	12%
Dietary Fiber	8.4g	30%
Total Sugars	16.2g	
Protein	5.1g	

Tips: Coconut milk is slightly fatter than other plant-based milk, but the medium chain triglycerides (MCTs) in coconuts have been linked to certain heart health benefits, such as lower HDL cholesterol levels.

Millet Salad with Spinach and Potatoes

Prep time: 10 min	Cook time: 30 min	Servings: 4

Ingredients

- *1.5 cups millet*
- *2.5 cups water*
- *7 oz. spinach finely chopped*
- *7 oz. potato, diced*
- *5.6 oz. chickpeas, canned*
- *14.1 oz. cucumber*
- *olive oil*
- *black pepper and salt*
- *1.4 oz. walnuts, finely chopped*

For the dressing

- *4 tbsp almond oil*

- *2 tbsp honey*
- *1 tbsp apple cider vinegar*
- *pepper and salt*

Directions

- Preheat the oven to 350°F. Meanwhile, bring some water to a boil.
- Add the millet and cook according to the package instructions.
- Cut the potato into pieces after peeling it. Wash and drain the chickpeas well and add to the potatoes, mix and place on a baking sheet. Bake for 20 min, stirring occasionally.
- Add spinach on top of the potato and chickpeas. Add a splash of olive oil and give everything a good shake. Bake for 10 min.
- Cut the cucumber into small cubes.
- Combine all the dressing ingredients, season to taste.
- Place the quinoa in a mixing bowl. Combine the roasted veggies, cucumber, and pecans in a mixing bowl. Toss in the dressing and mix well. If necessary, adjust the seasoning.

NUTRITION FACTS (PER SERVING)		
Calories	550	
Total Fat	17g	22%
Saturated Fat	2g	10%
Cholesterol	0mg	0%
Sodium	523mg	23%
Total Carbohydrate	84.5g	31%
Dietary Fiber	12.8g	46%
Total Sugars	14.4g	
Protein	18.4g	

Tips: Millet is a healthier alternative to rice since it contains significantly more protein and fiber.

Green Onion & Quinoa Soup

Prep time: 30 min	Cook time: 20 min	Servings: 4

Ingredients

- 2 green onions, white parts only, washed and thinly sliced
- ½ parsnips peeled cut into a small dice
- 1 tbsp olive oil
- 3 cups of water or broth
- ¼ cup quinoa
- Salt, to taste
- Freshly grated goat cheese

Directions

- In a large, heavy-based saucepan, heat olive oil over medium heat.
- Add the green onion, parsnips and 2 tbsp of water. Sprinkle with a little salt and sweat partially covered for 5 to 8 minutes or until the vegetables are tender.
- Add the remaining water. Lower the heat to medium-high and bring it to a boil. Add the quinoa and a generous pinch of salt.
- Bring the soup back to a boil, then cover the heat and reduce the heat to simmer for 20 minutes, stirring occasionally, until the quinoa is tender.
- Serve with plenty of freshly grated goat cheese.

NUTRITION FACTS (PER SERVING)

Calories	128	
Total Fat	5.4g	7%
Saturated Fat	1.3g	7%
Cholesterol	3mg	1%
Sodium	642mg	28%
Total Carbohydrate	13.8g	5%
Dietary Fiber	1.4g	5%
Total Sugars	2.7g	
Protein	6.2g	

Roasted Daikon Almonds Soup

Prep time: 10 min	Cook time: 40 min	Servings: 2

Ingredients

- 1 ½ lbs. daikon, peeled and cut into 1-inch pieces
- ½ cup chopped onion
- 3-4 cloves of garlic
- 3 tbsp sunflower oil
- Salt and black pepper to taste
- 4 cups chicken stock
- 1 tbsp grated ginger
- 1 cup almond milk
- 1 cup roasted almond, for garnish

- *Parsley leaves, for garnish*

Directions

- Preheat the oven to 400°F.
- Toss the daikon, onions and garlic with 2 tbsp sunflower oil on a baking sheet. Season with salt and pepper.
- Roast for 30 minutes, tossing periodically, until soft and browned in a preheated oven.
- Meanwhile, in a large skillet, heat the remaining 1 tbsp sunflower oil. Add the stock and ginger, reduce to low heat, and continue to cook until the daikon is done roasting.
- After the daikon and onions are roasted, add them to the stock mixture.
- Blend the soup with a blender until smooth.
- Return to the pan and stir in the milk. Bring to a boil.
- Serve in bowls with almond and chopped parsley on top.

NUTRITION FACTS (PER SERVING)

Calories	353	
Total Fat	3.3g	4%
Saturated Fat	1g	5%
Cholesterol	39mg	13%
Sodium	291mg	13%
Total Carbohydrate	48.5g	18%
Dietary Fiber	12.3g	44%
Total Sugars	2.9g	
Protein	33.2g	

Tips: Flour or corn starch can be used to thicken the soup. Never add flour or corn starch to your soup directly for the best results. It will clump up on top if you do so. Instead, spoon a tiny portion of the soup into a separate bowl and set it aside to cool.

Beet Hash

Prep time: 10 min	Cook time: 20 min	Servings: 2

Ingredients

- *2 large beets*
- *3 tbsp vegetable oil*
- *½ bell pepper chopped*
- *½ lb. chicken ground*
- *¼ cup leek, chopped*
- *½ cup carrot*
- *salt and black pepper*
- *2 tbsp freshly chopped basil*

Directions

- Microwave beets until they are cooked but not mushy. Peel the beets and chop them into little cubes.
- In a large skillet, heat 2 tbsp oil over medium-high heat and add bell pepper and carrot. Cook until the vegetables are soft. Break up the ground chicken until it is done. Add leeks, then cook for 1 more minute. Remove from the pan and place in a bowl to cool.
- In the same skillet, add the remaining oil and the beets in a single layer. Allow to cook for 5 minutes (uncovered) until golden brown, then mix and continue to boil until the beets are golden.
- Season with salt and pepper before adding the turkey mixture.
- Garnish with basil. If desired, put one or two fried eggs on top!

NUTRITION FACTS (PER SERVING)

Calories	398	
Total Fat	22.8g	29%
Saturated Fat	4.6g	23%
Cholesterol	63mg	21%
Sodium	132mg	6%
Total Carbohydrate	21g	8%
Dietary Fiber	3.9g	14%
Total Sugars	6.8g	
Protein	29g	

Tips: Beetroots provide substantial volumes of manganese, potassium, iron, and vitamin C, plus fiber, folate and other minerals.

Fresh Tarragon Turkey Salad

Prep time: 20 min	Cook time: 20 min	Servings: 4

Ingredients

- 1.5 lb. of turkey breast
- ½ salt (add more to taste, if needed)
- 2 tbsp grapeseed oil
- ¼–½ tsp of ground pepper
- 3–4 medium chopped carrot
- 1 pear
- 1 cup of coconut yogurt
- 1 tbsp of coconut yogurt or cream

- *1 tbsp of apple cider vinegar*
- *2–3 tbsp of fresh chopped tarragon*

Directions

- Preheat the oven to 450°F. Season both sides of the turkey breasts with salt and ground pepper after drizzling oil over them. Rub the turkey before spreading it out on a parchment-lined baking dish, roasting pan, or rimmed baking sheet.
- Bake for 15-20 minutes, or until the turkey reaches 165°F on the inside (no pink in the middle, juices running clear).
- Allow 5 minutes for the bird to rest before cutting it.
- Begin cutting the carrot and pear, as well as carefully chopping the fresh tarragon while the turkey is resting and cooling.
- In a medium mixing dish, combine the cut-up ingredients. After the turkey has cooled slightly, dice it and combine it with the remaining ingredients in your mixing dish.
- Season the salad to taste with salt and pepper, then chill for 10-15 minutes. Fresh herbs, chopped almonds, or pecans can be sprinkled over the top.

NUTRITION FACTS (PER SERVING)

Calories	160	
Total Fat	6.1g	8%
Saturated Fat	1.8g	9%
Cholesterol	25mg	8%
Sodium	412mg	18%
Total Carbohydrate	3.2g	1%
Dietary Fiber	0.5g	2%
Total Sugars	0.6g	
Protein	22.1g	

DESSERTS AND SMOOTHIES

Macadamia Peach Bars

Prep time: 30 min	Cook time: 35 min	Servings: 16

Ingredients

For the Dough

- 1 ½ cups almond flour
- ½ tsp baking powder
- ¼ tsp salt
- ½ tsp nutmeg
- ½ cup unsalted butter, cold (1 stick)
- 1 large egg

- *½ tsp vanilla extract*
- *½ cup coconut sugar, packed*
- *½ cup finely chopped macadamia nuts (+ more for topping)*

For the Filling

- *2 cups chopped peaches*
- *2 tbsp coconut sugar*
- *1 tbsp rice flour*

Directions

- Preheat the oven to 350°F. Set aside an 8-inch square pan lined with parchment paper.
- Combine flour, baking powder, salt, and nutmeg in a large mixing bowl. Cut in the butter with a fork, pastry cutter, or, in my case, my fingers until pea-sized crumbs form and the mixture resembles wet sand.
- Combine the egg, vanilla extract, coconut sugar, and chopped macadamia nuts in a mixing bowl. Make certain that everything is thoroughly blended.
- Set aside ⅓ of the mixture; pour the remaining ⅔ into the prepared pan and flatten with your hands into an equal layer.
- While you're making the filling, set the dough aside.
- Toss the peaches, coconut sugar, and rice flour together in a medium mixing basin until uniformly coated. Pour the mixture over the top of the crust and smooth it out evenly.
- Over the peaches, sprinkle the remaining ⅓ of the dough mixture. There's no need to be precise here; just make sure everything is on top.
- Bake for 35-37 minutes, or until the crust is golden and the fruit is bubbling, but not overly so. Allow to cool completely in the

pan before removing the bars from the parchment paper; otherwise, they will break apart.

- If preferred, top with more chopped Macadamia nuts before serving.

NUTRITION FACTS (PER SERVING)		
Calories	142	
Total Fat	7.6g	10%
Saturated Fat	3.9g	19%
Cholesterol	27mg	9%
Sodium	82mg	4%
Total Carbohydrate	16.9g	6%
Dietary Fiber	0.7g	3%
Total Sugars	7g	
Protein	2.1g	

Tips: Nuts are high in protein, healthy fats (polyunsaturated and monounsaturated), fiber, antioxidants, and a variety of vitamins and minerals.

Raspberries Sorbet

Prep time: 20 min	Cook time: 10 min	Servings: 4

Ingredients

- ½ cup water
- ⅓ cup coconut sugar
- 1 lb. fresh raspberries (stemmed)

Directions

- In a small saucepan over medium-high heat, combine water and coconut sugar.
- As the water heats up, whisk it, and when it boils and the coconut sugar dissolves, cook for another minute while whisking. Remove from the heat.

- Allow 5 minutes for the coconut sugar solution to cool.
- Place the raspberries and the coconut sugar solution in a blender and blend until smooth.
- For 1 minute, pulse the blender in 10-second bursts.
- Fill a plastic storage container halfway with the raspberry mixture.
- Fill the container with ice and place it in the freezer. Whisk the mixture vigorously every 7 to 10 minutes.
- Switch to a rubber spatula as the mixture thickens until the sorbet is completely frozen.

NUTRITION FACTS (PER SERVING)		
Calories	99	
Total Fat	0.3g	0%
Saturated Fat	0g	0%
Cholesterol	0mg	0%
Sodium	2mg	0%
Total Carbohydrate	25.4g	9%
Dietary Fiber	2.3g	8%
Total Sugars	22.2g	
Protein	0.8g	

Tips: To make sorbet at home, add 4 cups fruit purée or juice (approximately 5-6 cups slices or pieces), 1 cup sugar, and 2-4 tbsps acid of your choice, plus a tsp of salt in a mixing bowl. You may need up to 2 cups of simple syrup if using it, but start with less and work your way up. This is the sorbet master ratio.

<u>Maple Syrup Yogurt Sauce</u>

| Prep time: 20 min | Cook time: 10 min | Servings: 2 |

Ingredients

- *¼ cup Greek non-fat yogurt*
- *1 tsp maple syrup*
- *1 tsp mango juice*

Directions

- Combine the yogurt, maple syrup, and mango juice in a mixing bowl.
- Before serving, chill well.

NUTRITION FACTS (PER SERVING)

Calories	55	
Total Fat	0g	0%
Saturated Fat	0g	0%
Cholesterol	1mg	0%
Sodium	27mg	1%
Total Carbohydrate	9.8g	4%
Dietary Fiber	0g	0%
Total Sugars	9g	
Protein	4.8g	

Tips: Yogurt is mostly made up of milk. Whole milk for full-fat yogurt, low-fat milk for low-fat yogurt, and skim milk for non-fat yogurt — the type of milk used depends on the type of yogurt.

Dairy-Free Rice Pudding

Prep time: 40 min	Cook time: 15 min	Servings: 6

Ingredients

- ½ cup rice
- ½ cup water
- 1½ cups unsweetened coconut milk
- 1 tsp nutmeg
- ¼ cup chopped fig
- ¼ cup maple syrup
- ½ tsp vanilla extract
- ½ cup sliced walnut

Directions

- Put the rice in a colander and rinse with water. Drain for a few minutes.

- Put the rice in a large saucepan and add the water and coconut milk. Bring to a boil over medium heat.
- Simmer and cook for 30 minutes, stirring frequently to avoid sticking.
- Add the fig, maple syrup and vanilla extract. Stir to combine and remove from heat.
- Let cool to room temperature or put it in a cool place. If the pudding gets too thick, add more coconut milk as needed.
- Serve with flaked walnuts.

NUTRITION FACTS (PER SERVING)

Calories	400	
Total Fat	11.2g	14%
Saturated Fat	1g	5%
Cholesterol	0mg	0%
Sodium	142mg	6%
Total Carbohydrate	69.6g	25%
Dietary Fiber	6.3g	22%
Total Sugars	34.6g	
Protein	9.9g	

Tips: Fiber is great for you as it may lower cholesterol and reduce the risk of heart disease and stroke.

Orange Yogurt Pops

Prep time: 20 min	Cook time: 10 min	Servings: 4

Ingredients

- ½ cup non-fat yogurt
- ¼ cup ricotta cheese
- ¼ cup coconut sugar
- ¼ cup orange juice

Directions

- In a blender, combine non-fat yogurt, ricotta cheese, coconut sugar, and orange juice. Puree until completely smooth.

- Place sticks in each pop after pouring into freezer pop molds. Freeze for a minimum of 3 hours.
- When ready to serve, run the plastic molds under hot water, making sure the frozen pop does not get any water inside. Depending on the sort of mold you use, loosening the pops will only take 5 to 10 seconds.
- Serve and enjoy!

NUTRITION FACTS (PER SERVING)		
Calories	60	
Total Fat	0.3g	0%
Saturated Fat	0.2g	1%
Cholesterol	3mg	1%
Sodium	117mg	5%
Total Carbohydrate	10.7g	4%
Dietary Fiber	0g	0%
Total Sugars	5.8g	
Protein	3.3g	

Tips: Combine yogurt and berries or chopped fruits in a bowl (if using). Fill popsicle molds halfway with yogurt. Place the popsicle molds in the freezer and keep them there until they are hardened (at least 3 hours, I usually freeze them overnight). Place the popsicle in warm running water for a few seconds to release it from the mold.

Acid Reflux Smoothie

Prep time: 10 min	Cook time: 0 min	Servings: 1

Ingredients

- ¾ cup rice milk
- 5 fresh basil leaves
- ¼ cup fresh kale
- ½ tsp ginger powder
- 1 banana
- ½ apple
- ⅓ cup quinoa

Directions

- Put all the ingredients in a blender.
- Blend until smooth.

- For a refreshingly chilled smoothie, serve over ice.

NUTRITION FACTS (PER SERVING)

Calories	273	
Total Fat	3.9g	5%
Saturated Fat	0.4g	2%
Cholesterol	0mg	0%
Sodium	130mg	6%
Total Carbohydrate	57.5g	21%
Dietary Fiber	8.4g	30%
Total Sugars	21.6g	
Protein	5.7g	

Tips: Small amounts of water, milk, or juice can be added. Increase the speed of your machine to its highest setting and process for 10-20 seconds.

Kale & Strawberry Smoothie

Prep time: 5 min	Cook time: 0 min	Servings: 1

Ingredients

- ¼ avocado
- 1 cup baby kale
- 1 cup frozen strawberries
- ½ cup rice milk
- 1 tbsp pumpkin seeds
- 1 cup ice

Directions

- Put all the ingredients in a blender.

117

- Blend until smooth.
- Serve immediately and enjoy!

NUTRITION FACTS (PER SERVING)

Calories	254	
Total Fat	15.4g	20%
Saturated Fat	12.9g	64%
Cholesterol	0mg	0%
Sodium	32mg	1%
Total Carbohydrate	30.8g	11%
Dietary Fiber	5.8g	21%
Total Sugars	17.6g	
Protein	3.7g	

Tips: Due to its high concentration of vitamins, minerals, and antioxidants, kale is one of the healthiest vegetables on the Earth. Despite its high goitrogens content, research reveals that consuming raw kale in moderation has little effect on thyroid health.

Chervil Smoothie

Prep time: 10 min	Cook time: 0 min	Servings: 2

Ingredients

- ½ bunch of chervil with stems cut
- 2 small apples, cored
- 1 cup coconut water
- ¾ cup banana, peeled

Directions

- Put all the ingredients in a blender.
- Blend until smooth.

119

- Serve and enjoy!

NUTRITION FACTS (PER SERVING)

Calories	316	
Total Fat	24.7g	32%
Saturated Fat	21.5g	107%
Cholesterol	0mg	0%
Sodium	24mg	1%
Total Carbohydrate	26.4g	10%
Dietary Fiber	5.9g	21%
Total Sugars	17.2g	
Protein	3.9g	

Tips: A smoothie mixed with water is your best bet if you're seeking to reduce your calorie and sugar intake. If you want a creamy and not-too-sweet smoothie, milk is the way to go.

Spinach Smoothie

Prep time: 5 min	Cook time: 0 min	Servings: 1

Ingredients

- *1 cup spinach*
- *1 cup diced apple*
- *¼ avocado*
- *1 cup water*
- *1 tbsp pumpkin seeds*

Directions

- Put all the ingredients in a blender.
- Blend until smooth.
- Serve immediately and enjoy!

NUTRITION FACTS (PER SERVING)

Calories	267	
Total Fat	2.9g	4%
Saturated Fat	0.5g	2%
Cholesterol	0mg	0%
Sodium	42mg	2%
Total Carbohydrate	61.1g	22%
Dietary Fiber	9.2g	33%
Total Sugars	31.4g	
Protein	5.7g	

Tips: Avocados include riboflavin, folate, pantothenic acid, magnesium and potassium and vitamins C, E, K, and B-6, all great for your health

Spinach Papaya Superfood Smoothie

Prep time: 5 min	Cook time: 0 min	Servings: 8

Ingredients

- *8 cups spinach packed*
- *6 cups soy milk*
- *6 cups papaya chunks*
- *1 tsp vanilla extract*

Directions

- Add all ingredients into a blender.
- Blend until smooth and creamy.
- Pour into glasses and enjoy.

NUTRITION FACTS (PER SERVING)

Calories	173	
Total Fat	5.2g	7%
Saturated Fat	0.6g	3%
Cholesterol	0mg	0%
Sodium	127mg	6%
Total Carbohydrate	24.9g	9%
Dietary Fiber	3.8g	14%
Total Sugars	16g	
Protein	8.3g	

Tips: People who are trying to lose weight often skip their morning meals and eat large amounts between meals. To avoid this, experts recommend smoothies made with excellent fruits and flavors to keep you full for a long time.

Peaches Cantaloupe Smoothie

Prep time: 10 min	Cook time: 0 min	Servings: 2

Ingredients

- *2 cups cantaloupe, peeled, seeded and cut into chunks*
- *4 tbsp fresh aloe vera*
- *1 peach, peeled, cored and cut in half*
- *⅛ tsp. lemon zest*
- *1 ½ cups ice*
- *¼ tsp salt, to taste*

Directions

- Put all the ingredients in a blender.

- Blend until smooth.
- Serve and enjoy!

NUTRITION FACTS (PER SERVING)

Calories	165	
Total Fat	1g	1%
Saturated Fat	0.2g	1%
Cholesterol	0mg	0%
Sodium	50mg	2%
Total Carbohydrate	39.5g	14%
Dietary Fiber	5.1g	18%
Total Sugars	38.5g	
Protein	4g	

Tips: Cantaloupe is abundant in many minerals and vitamins. Among them are potassium and vitamin C. Eating it on a regular basis may contribute to your heart health and may lower your bad cholesterol levels.

Watermelon Smoothie with Orange

Prep time: 10 min	Cook time: 0 min	Servings: 1

Ingredients

- *1 cup watermelon, cut into chunks*
- *1 handful raspberries*
- *juice of half an orange*
- *fresh basil*

Directions

- Put all the ingredients in a blender.
- Blend until smooth.
- Serve and enjoy!

NUTRITION FACTS (PER SERVING)

Calories	430	
Total Fat	33g	42%
Saturated Fat	29g	145%
Cholesterol	0mg	0%
Sodium	81mg	4%
Total Carbohydrate	37g	13%
Dietary Fiber	9g	32%
Total Sugars	18.5g	
Protein	4.6g	

Tips: Fill the container with liquids first, followed by soft fruits or vegetables, greens, and ice on top.

2-WEEKS MEAL PLAN

1st Week

Day	Breakfast	Lunch	Dinner	Dessert
1	Pears Pancakes	Grilled Chicken Veggie Burgers	Marjoram Lamb	Orange Yogurt Pops
2	French Toast	Turkey, Quinoa & Vegetable Soup	Sweet Potato Sorghum	Dairy-Free Rice Pudding
3	Couscous and Pears Breakfast Porridge	Cashew Turkey	Roasted Daikon Almonds Soup	Watermelon Smoothie with Orange
4	Sprouted Millet Crepes	Couscous Crusted Mackerel	Honey Tarragon Chicken Breasts	Maple Syrup Yogurt Sauce
5	Almond Coconut Granola	Asian Tempeh	Milled Salad with Sweet Potatoes	Peaches and Cantaloupe Smoothie
6	Beets Bread	Pears Pie Beef	Fresh Tarragon Turkey Salad	Raspberries Sorbet
7	Breakfast Barley with Pomegranates	Beef Tenderloin and Butternut Squash	Coconut Parsnips Soup	Macadamia Peach Bars

2nd Week

Day	Breakfast	Lunch	Dinner	Dessert
1	Fruity and Healthy Barley	Green Onion & Quinoa Soup	Trout Mac and Cheese	Macadamia Peach Bars
2	Warming Blackberries Porridge	Smoked Black Beans Spinach Stir Fry	Orange Marjoram Lamb	Raspberries Sorbet
3	Beets Bread	Coconut Parsnips Soup	Roasted Daikon Almonds Soup	Peaches and Cantaloupe Smoothie
4	Couscous and Pears Breakfast Porridge	Milled Salad with Spinach and Potatoes	Beet Hash	Spinach Smoothie
5	Sprouted Milled Crepes	Beef Tenderloin and Butternut Squash	Lentil and Cannellini Bean Soup	Orange Yogurt Pops
6	French Toast	One-Skillet Chicken in Mushroom Sauce	Fish Soup with Sweet Potatoes	Maple Syrup Yogurt Sauce
7	Baked Apricots Hazelnuts Buckwheat	Grilled Chicken Veggie Burgers	Honey Tarragon Chicken Breasts	Watermelon Smoothie with Orange

Printed in Great Britain
by Amazon

16690596R00078